Key Facts™ on

Myanmar (Burma)

~Essential Information on Myanmar~

By Patrick W. Nee

The Internationalist®
www.internationalist.com

The Internationalist®

International Business, Investment, and Travel

Published by:

The Internationalist Publishing Company

96 Walter Street/ Suite 200

Boston, MA 02131, USA

Tel: 617-354-7722

www.internationalist.com

PN@internationalist.com

Copyright © 2013 by PWN

The Internationalist is a Registered Trademark. "Key Facts" and "The Internationalist Business Guides" are Trademarks of The Internationalist Publishing Company.

All Rights are reserved under International, Pan-American, and Pan-Asian Conventions. No part of this book may be reproduced in any form without the written permission of the publisher. All rights vigorously enforced

Table Of Contents

Chapter 1: Background

Chapter 2: Geography

Chapter 3: People and Society

Chapter 4: Government and Key Leaders

Chapter 5: Economy

Chapter 6: Energy

Chapter 7: Communications

Chapter 8: Transportation

Chapter 9: Military

Chapter 10: Transnational Issues

Map of Myanmar (Burma)

Chapter 1: Background

Various ethnic Burmese and ethnic minority city-states or kingdoms occupied the present borders through the 19th century. Over a period of 62 years (1824-1886), Britain conquered Burma and incorporated the country into its Indian Empire. Burma was administered as a province of India until 1937 when it became a separate, self-governing colony; in 1948, Burma attained independence from the Commonwealth. Gen. NE WIN dominated the government from 1962 to 1988, first as military ruler, then as self-appointed president, and later as political kingpin. In response to widespread civil unrest, NE WIN resigned in 1988, but within months the military crushed student-led protests and took power. Multiparty legislative elections in 1990 resulted in the main opposition party - the National League for Democracy (NLD) - winning a landslide victory. Instead of handing over power, the junta placed NLD leader (and Nobel Peace Prize recipient) AUNG SAN SUU KYI (ASSK) under house arrest from 1989 to 1995, 2000 to 2002, and from May 2003 to November 2010. In late September 2007, the ruling junta brutally suppressed protests over increased fuel prices led by prodemocracy activists and Buddhist monks, killing at least 13 people and arresting thousands for participating in the demonstrations. In early May 2008, Burma was struck by Cyclone Nargis, which left over 138,000 dead and tens of thousands injured and homeless. Despite this tragedy, the junta proceeded with its May constitutional referendum, the first vote in Burma since 1990. Parliamentary elections held in November 2010, considered flawed by many in the international community, saw the ruling Union Solidarity and Development Party garner over 75% of the seats. Parliament convened in January 2011 and selected former Prime Minister THEIN SEIN as president. Although the vast majority of national-level appointees named by THEIN SEIN are former or current military officers, the government has initiated a series of political and economic reforms leading to a substantial opening of the long-isolated country. These reforms have included allowing ASSK to contest parliamentary by-elections on 1 April 2012, releasing hundreds of political prisoners, reaching preliminary peace agreements with 10 of the 11 major armed ethnic groups, enacting laws that provide better protections for basic human rights, and gradually reducing restrictions on freedom of the press, association, and civil society. At least due in part to these reforms, ASSK now serves as an elected Member of Parliament and chair of the Committee for Rule of Law and Tranquility. Most political parties have begun building their institutions in preparation for the next round of general elections in 2015. The country is preparing to chair the Association of Southeast Asian Nations (ASEAN) in 2014.

Chapter 2: Geography

Location:
Southeastern Asia, bordering the Andaman Sea and the Bay of Bengal, between Bangladesh and Thailand

Geographic coordinates:
22 00 N, 98 00 E

Map references:
Southeast Asia

Area:
total: 676,578 sq km
country comparison to the world: 40
land: 653,508 sq km
water: 23,070 sq km

Area - comparative:
slightly smaller than Texas

Land boundaries:
total: 5,876 km
border countries: Bangladesh 193 km, China 2,185 km, India 1,463 km, Laos 235 km, Thailand 1,800 km

Coastline:
1,930 km

Maritime claims:
territorial sea: 12 nm

contiguous zone: 24 nm

exclusive economic zone: 200 nm

continental shelf: 200 nm or to the edge of the continental margin

Climate:

tropical monsoon; cloudy, rainy, hot, humid summers (southwest monsoon, June to September); less cloudy, scant rainfall, mild temperatures, lower humidity during winter (northeast monsoon, December to April)

Terrain:

central lowlands ringed by steep, rugged highlands

Elevation extremes:

lowest point: Andaman Sea 0 m

highest point: Hkakabo Razi 5,881 m

Natural resources:

petroleum, timber, tin, antimony, zinc, copper, tungsten, lead, coal, marble, limestone, precious stones, natural gas, hydropower

Land use:

arable land: 15.94%

permanent crops: 2.16%

other: 81.89% (2011)

Irrigated land:

21,100 sq km (2004)
Total renewable water resources:
1,168 cu km (2011)
Freshwater withdrawal (domestic/industrial/agricultural):
total: 33.23 cu km/yr (10%/1%/89%)
per capita: 728.6 cu m/yr (2005)
Natural hazards:
destructive earthquakes and cyclones; flooding and landslides common during rainy season (June to September); periodic droughts
Environment - current issues:
deforestation; industrial pollution of air, soil, and water; inadequate sanitation and water treatment contribute to disease
Environment - international agreements:
party to: Biodiversity, Climate Change, Climate Change-Kyoto Protocol, Desertification, Endangered Species, Law of the Sea, Ozone Layer Protection, Ship Pollution, Tropical Timber 83, Tropical Timber 94
signed, but not ratified: none of the selected agreements
Geography - note:

strategic location near major Indian Ocean shipping lanes

Chapter 3: People and Society

Nationality:
>noun: Burmese (singular and plural)
>
>adjective: Burmese

Ethnic groups:
>Burman 68%, Shan 9%, Karen 7%, Rakhine 4%, Chinese 3%, Indian 2%, Mon 2%, other 5%

Languages:
>Burmese (official)
>
>note: minority ethnic groups have their own languages

Religions:
>Buddhist 89%, Christian 4% (Baptist 3%, Roman Catholic 1%), Muslim 4%, Animist 1%, other 2%

Population:
>55,167,330 (July 2013 est.)
>
>country comparison to the world: 24
>
>note: estimates for this country take into account the effects of excess mortality due to AIDS; this can result in lower life expectancy, higher infant mortality, higher death rates, lower population growth rates, and changes in the distribution of population by age and sex than would otherwise be expected

Age structure:
    0-14 years: 26.7% (male 7,514,233/female 7,227,893)
    15-24 years: 18.6% (male 5,183,653/female 5,060,385)
    25-54 years: 42.8% (male 11,724,297/female 11,879,420)
    55-64 years: 6.7% (male 1,754,397/female 1,963,051)
    65 years and over: 5.2% (male 1,244,758/female 1,615,243) (2013 est.)

Median age:
    total: 27.6 years
    male: 27 years
    female: 28.2 years (2013 est.)

Population growth rate:
    1.05% (2013 est.)
    country comparison to the world: 109

Birth rate:
    18.89 births/1,000 population (2013 est.)
    country comparison to the world: 96

Death rate:
    8.05 deaths/1,000 population (2013 est.)
    country comparison to the world: 95

Net migration rate:
    -0.3 migrant(s)/1,000 population (2013 est.)

country comparison to the world: 123

Urbanization:
urban population: 32.6% of total population (2011)
rate of urbanization: 2.49% annual rate of change (2010-15 est.)

Major urban areas - population:
RANGOON (capital) 4.259 million; Mandalay 1.009 million; Nay Pyi Taw 992,000 (2009)

Sex ratio:
at birth: 1.06 male(s)/female
0-14 years: 1.04 male(s)/female
15-24 years: 1.02 male(s)/female
25-54 years: 0.99 male(s)/female
55-64 years: 0.9 male(s)/female
65 years and over: 0.77 male(s)/female
total population: 0.99 male(s)/female (2013 est.)

Maternal mortality rate:
200 deaths/100,000 live births (2010)
country comparison to the world: 52

Infant mortality rate:
total: 46.31 deaths/1,000 live births
country comparison to the world: 46
male: 52.91 deaths/1,000 live births
female: 39.31 deaths/1,000 live births (2013 est.)

Life expectancy at birth:
    total population: 65.6 years
    country comparison to the world: 170
    male: 63.24 years
    female: 68.09 years (2013 est.)

Total fertility rate:
    2.21 children born/woman (2013 est.)
    country comparison to the world: 102

Contraceptive prevalence rate:
    46% (2009/10)

Health expenditures:
    2% of GDP (2010)
    country comparison to the world: 190

Physicians density:
    0.46 physicians/1,000 population (2008)

Hospital bed density:
    0.6 beds/1,000 population (2006)

Drinking water source:
    improved:
        urban: 93% of population
        rural: 78% of population
        total: 83% of population
    unimproved:
        urban: 7% of population

rural: 22% of population
total: 17% of population (2010 est.)

Sanitation facility access:
improved:
urban: 83% of population
rural: 73% of population
total: 76% of population
unimproved:
urban: 17% of population
rural: 27% of population
total: 24% of population (2010 est.)

HIV/AIDS - adult prevalence rate:
0.6% (2009 est.)
country comparison to the world: 64

HIV/AIDS - people living with HIV/AIDS:
240,000 (2009 est.)
country comparison to the world: 24

HIV/AIDS - deaths:
18,000 (2009 est.)
country comparison to the world: 17

Major infectious diseases:
degree of risk: very high
food or waterborne diseases: bacterial and protozoal diarrhea, hepatitis A, and typhoid fever

vectorborne diseases: dengue fever, malaria, and Japanese encephalitis

water contact disease: leptospirosis

animal contact disease: rabies

note: highly pathogenic H5N1 avian influenza has been identified in this country; it poses a negligible risk with extremely rare cases possible among US citizens who have close contact with birds (2013)

Obesity - adult prevalence rate:

4% (2008)

country comparison to the world: 172

Children under the age of 5 years underweight:

22.6% (2010)

country comparison to the world: 26

Education expenditures:

0.8% of GDP (2011)

country comparison to the world: 172

Literacy:

definition: age 15 and over can read and write

total population: 89.9%

male: 93.9%

female: 86.4% (2006 est.)

School life expectancy (primary to tertiary education):

total: 9 years (2007)

Chapter 4: Government and Key Leaders

Country name:

    <u>conventional long form</u>: Union of Burma

    <u>conventional short form</u>: Burma

    <u>local long form</u>: Pyidaungzu Myanma Naingngandaw (translated by the US Government as Union of Myanma and by the Burmese as Union of Myanmar)

    <u>local short form</u>: Myanma Naingngandaw

    <u>former</u>: Socialist Republic of the Union of Burma

    <u>note</u>: since 1989 the military authorities in Burma, and the current parliamentary government, have promoted the name Myanmar as a conventional name for their state; the US Government has not adopted the name, which is a derivative of the Burmese short-form name Myanma Naingngandaw

Government type:

    parliamentary government took power in March 2011

Capital:

    <u>name</u>: Rangoon (Yangon)

    <u>geographic coordinates</u>: 16 48 N, 96 09 E

    <u>time difference</u>: UTC+6.5 (11.5 hours ahead of Washington, DC during Standard Time)

    <u>note</u>: Nay Pyi Taw is the administrative capital

Administrative divisions:
>7 regions (taing-myar, singular - taing) and 7 states (pyi ne-myar, singular - pyi ne)
>regions: Ayeyarwady, Bago, Magway, Mandalay, Sagaing, Taninthayi, Yangon
>states: Chin, Kachin, Kayah, Kayin, Mon, Rakhine (Arakan), Shan
>union territory: Nay Pyi Taw

Independence:
>4 January 1948 (from the UK)

National holiday:
>Independence Day, 4 January (1948); Union Day, 12 February (1947)

Constitution:
>approved by referendum 29 May 2008; reformed by a series of acts in 2011

Legal system:
>mixed legal system of English common law (as introduced in codifications designed for colonial India) and customary law

International law organization participation:
>has not submitted an ICJ jurisdiction declaration; non-party state to the ICCt

Suffrage:

18 years of age; universal

Executive branch:

chief of state: President THEIN SEIN (since 4 February 2011); Vice President SAI MOUK KHAM (since 3 February 2011); Vice President NYAN HTUN (since 15 August 2012)

head of government: President THEIN SEIN (since 4 February 2011)

cabinet: cabinet is appointed by the president and confirmed by the parliament

elections: THEIN SEIN elected president by the parliament from among three vice presidents; the upper house, the lower house, and military members of the parliament each nominate one vice president (president serves a five-year term)

Legislative branch:

bicameral, consists of the House of Nationalities [Amyotha Hluttaw] (224 seats, 168 directly elected and 56 appointed by the military; members serve five-year terms) and the House of Representatives [Pythu Hluttaw] (440 seats, 330 directly elected and 110 appointed by the military; members serve five-year terms) elections: last held on 7 November 2010 (next to be held in December 2015)

election results: House of Nationalities - percent of vote by party - USDP 74.8%, others (NUP, SNDP, RNDP, NDF, AMRDP) 25.2%; seats by party - USDP 129, others 39; House of Representatives - percent of vote by party - USDP 79.6%, others (NUP, SNDP, RNDP, NDF, AMRDP) 20.4%; seats by party - USDP 259, others 71

Judicial branch:

highest court(s): Supreme Court of the Union (consists of the chief justice and 7-11 judges)

judge selection and term of office: chief justice and judges nominated by the president and approved by the Pythu Hlattaw; judges normally serve until mandatory retirement at age 70

subordinate courts: High Courts of the Region; High Courts of the State; Court of the Self-Administered Division; Court of the Self-Administered Zone; district and township courts; special courts (for juvenile, municipal, and traffic offenses); courts martial

Political parties and leaders:

All Mon Region Democracy Party or AMRDP [NAING NGWE THEIN]
National Democratic Force or NDF [KHIN MAUNG SWE, Dr.THAN NYEIN]
National League for Democracy or NLD [AUNG SAN SUU KYI]
National Unity Party or NUP [TUN YE]
Rakhine Nationalities Development Party or RNDP [Dr. AYE MG]
Shan Nationalities Democratic Party or SNDP [SAI AIKE PAUNG]
Shan Nationalities League for Democracy or SNLD [HKUN HTUN OO]
Union Solidarity and Development Party or USDP [SHWE MANN, HTAY OO]
numerous smaller parties

Political pressure groups and leaders:

Thai border:
Ethnic Nationalities Council or ENC
Federation of Trade Unions-Burma or FTUB (exile trade union and labor advocates)
National Coalition Government of the Union of Burma or NCGUB (self-proclaimed government in exile) ["Prime Minister" Dr. SEIN WIN] consists of

individuals, some legitimately elected to the People's Assembly in 1990 (the group fled to a border area and joined insurgents in December 1990 to form a parallel government in exile)

National Council-Union of Burma or NCUB (exile coalition of opposition groups)

United Nationalities Federal Council (UNFC)

<u>Inside Burma</u>:

Karen National Union or KNU

Karenni National People's Party or KNPP

United Wa State Army or UWSA

88 Generation Students (pro-democracy movement)

several other Chin, Karen, Mon, and Shan factions

<u>note</u>: freedom of expression has been highly restricted in Burma; the restrictions are being relaxed by the government; political groups, other than parties approved by the government, are limited in number

International organization participation:

ADB, ARF, ASEAN, BIMSTEC, CP, EAS, FAO, G-77, IAEA, IBRD, ICAO, ICRM, IDA, IFAD, IFC, IFRCS, IHO, ILO, IMF, IMO, Interpol, IOC, IOM, IPU, ISO (correspondent), ITU, ITUC (NGOs), NAM, OPCW (signatory), SAARC (observer), UN,

UNCTAD, UNESCO, UNIDO, UNWTO, UPU, WCO, WHO, WIPO, WMO, WTO

Diplomatic representation in the US:

chief of mission: Ambassador THAN SWE

chancery: 2300 S Street NW, Washington, DC 20008

telephone: [1] (202) 332-3344

FAX: [1] (202) 332-4351

consulate(s) general: none; Burma has a Mission to the UN in New York

Diplomatic representation from the US:

chief of mission: Ambassador Derek J. MITCHELL

embassy: 110 University Avenue, Kamayut Township, Rangoon

mailing address: Box B, APO AP 96546

telephone: [95] (1) 536 509, 535-756, 538-038

FAX: [95] (1) 511-069

Key Leaders:

Pres.	THEIN SEIN
Vice Pres.	NYAN TUN
Vice Pres.	SAI MAUK KHAM, *Dr.*
Min. for Agriculture & Irrigation	MYINT HLAING
Min. for Border Affairs	THEIN HTAY, *Maj. Gen.*

Min. of Commerce	WIN MYINT
Min. of Communications, Post, & Telegraph	THEIN TUN
Min. of Construction	KYAW LWIN
Min. for Cooperatives	KYAW HSAN
Min. of Culture	AYE MYINT KYU
Min. of Defense	WAI LWIN, *Lt. Gen.*
Min. of Education	MYA AYE
Min. of Electric Power	KHIN MAUNG SOE
Min. of Energy	THAN HTAY
Min. of Environmental Conservation & Forestry	WIN TUN
Min. of Finance & Revenue	WIN SHEIN
Min. of Foreign Affairs	WUNNA MAUNG LWIN
Min. of Health	PE THET KHIN, *Dr.*
Min. of Home Affairs	KO KO, *Lt. Gen.*
Min. of Hotels & Tourism	HTAY AUNG
Min. of Immigration &	KHIN YI

Population	
Min. of Industry	AYE MYINT
Min. of Information	AUNG KYI
Min. of Labor	MAUNG MYINT
Min. of Livestock & Fisheries	OHN MYINT
Min. of Mines	MYINT AUNG
Min. of National Planning & Economic Development	KAN ZAW
Min. of Rail Transport	ZEYAR AUNG
Min. of Religious Affairs	MYINT MAUNG
Min. of Science & Technology	KO KO OO
Min. of Social Welfare, Relief, & Resettlement	MYAT MYAT OHN KHIN
Min. of Sports	TINT HSAN
Min. for Transport	NYAN TUN AUNG
Min. in the Office of the Pres.	AUNG MIN
Min. in the Office of the Pres.	HLA TUN

Min. in the Office of the Pres.	SOE MAUNG
Min. in the Office of the Pres.	SOE THEIN
Min. in the Office of the Pres.	THEIN NYUNT
Min. in the Office of the Pres.	TIN NAING THEIN
Governor, Central Bank of Burma	THAN NYEIN
Ambassador to the US	THAN SWE
Permanent Representative to the UN, New York	TIN KYAW

Flag description:

design consists of three equal horizontal stripes of yellow (top), green, and red; centered on the green band is a large white five-pointed star that partially overlaps onto the adjacent colored stripes; the design revives the triband colors used by Burma from 1943-45, during the Japanese occupation

National symbol(s):

chinthe (mythical lion)

National anthem:

name: "Kaba Ma Kyei" (Till the End of the World, Myanmar)

lyrics/music: SAYA TIN

note: adopted 1948; Burma is among a handful of non-European nations that have anthems rooted in indigenous traditions; the beginning portion of the anthem is a traditional Burmese anthem before transitioning into a Western-style orchestrated work

Chapter 5: Economy

Economy - overview:

Burma is a resource-rich country but still suffers from pervasive government controls, inefficient economic policies, corruption, and rural poverty. Burma is the poorest country in Southeast Asia; approximately 32% of the population lives in poverty. Corruption is prevalent and significant resources are concentrated in the extractive industries are concentrated in a few hands. The Burmese government has initiated notable economic reforms. In October 2011, 11 private banks were allowed to trade foreign currency. On April 2, 2012, Burma's multiple exchange rates were abolished and the Central Bank of Myanmar established a managed float of the Burmese kyat. In November 2012, President THEIN SEIN signed a new Foreign Investment Law. Despite these reforms, the Burmese government has not yet embarked on broad-based macro-economic reforms or addressed key impediments to economic development such as Burma's opaque revenue collection system. Key benchmarks of economic progress would include steps to ensure the independence of the Central Bank, provide budget allocation for social services, and enact laws to protect intellectual and real property. In recent years, foreign investors have shied away from nearly every sector except for natural gas, power generation, timber, and mining. The exploitation of natural resources does not benefit the population at large. The most productive sectors will continue to be in extractive industries - especially oil and gas, mining, and timber - with the latter two causing significant environmental degradation. Other areas, such as manufacturing, tourism, and services, struggle in the face of poor infrastructure, unpredictable trade policies, undeveloped human resources (the result of neglected health and education systems), endemic corruption, and inadequate access to capital for investment. The US initially imposed sanctions on Burma in response to the 1988 military crackdown and the regime's refusal to honor the democratic opposition National League for Democracy's 1990 landslide election victory under the leadership of AUNG SAN SUU KYI. In 2003, the US moved from broad-based to more targeted sanctions. In July 2012, as a result of reforms undertaken by President THEIN SEIN and his nominally civilian government, the US broadly eased restrictions on new investment in and the export of financial services to Burma. In November 2012, the US eased the import bank on Burmese products to the US with the exception of jadeite and rubies. Although the Burmese government has good economic relations with its neighbors, significant improvements in economic governance, the business climate, and the political situation are needed to promote serious foreign investment.

GDP (purchasing power parity):

$90.93 billion (2012 est.)

country comparison to the world: 77

$85.54 billion (2011 est.)

$81.11 billion (2010 est.)

note: data are in 2012 US dollars

GDP (official exchange rate):

$53.14 billion (2012 est.)

GDP - real growth rate:

6.3% (2012 est.)

country comparison to the world: 42

5.5% (2011 est.)

5.3% (2010 est.)

GDP - per capita (PPP):

$1,400 (2012 est.)

country comparison to the world: 206
$1,400 (2011 est.)
$1,300 (2010 est.)
note: data are in 2012 US dollars

GDP - composition by sector:
agriculture: 38.8%
industry: 19.3%
services: 41.8% (2012 est.)

Labor force:
33.41 million (2012 est.)
country comparison to the world: 19

Labor force - by occupation:
agriculture: 70%
industry: 7%
services: 23% (2001)

Unemployment rate:
5.4% (2012 est.)
country comparison to the world: 51
5.5% (2011 est.)

Population below poverty line:
32.7% (2007 est.)

Household income or consumption by percentage share:
lowest 10%: 2.8%
highest 10%: 32.4% (1998)

Investment (gross fixed):
16.3% of GDP (2012 est.)
country comparison to the world: 128

Budget:
revenues: $2.271 billion
expenditures: $4.487 billion (2012 est.)

Taxes and other revenues:
4.3% of GDP (2012 est.)
country comparison to the world: 215

Budget surplus (+) or deficit (-):
-4.2% of GDP (2012 est.)
country comparison to the world: 151

Inflation rate (consumer prices):
1.5% (2012 est.)
country comparison to the world: 29
5% (2011 est.)

Central bank discount rate:
9.95% (31 December 2010 est.)
country comparison to the world: 18
12% (31 December 2009 est.)

Commercial bank prime lending rate:
13% (31 December 2012 est.)
country comparison to the world: 32
16.33% (31 December 2011 est.)

Stock of narrow money:

$11.54 million (31 December 2012 est.)

country comparison to the world: 190

$8.91 million (31 December 2011 est.)

Stock of domestic credit:

$15.66 billion (31 December 2011 est.)

country comparison to the world: 90

$11.83 billion (31 December 2010 est.)

Market value of publicly traded shares:

$NA

Agriculture - products:

rice, pulses, beans, sesame, groundnuts, sugarcane; fish and fish products; hardwood

Industries:

agricultural processing; wood and wood products; copper, tin, tungsten, iron; cement, construction materials; pharmaceuticals; fertilizer; oil and natural gas; garments, jade and gems

Industrial production growth rate:

8.6% (2012 est.)

country comparison to the world: 18

Current account balance:

-$891.2 million (2012 est.)

country comparison to the world: 108

$96.1 million (2011 est.)

Exports:

$8.23 billion (2012 est.)

country comparison to the world: 100

$8.113 billion (2011 est.)

note: official export figures are grossly underestimated due to the value of timber, gems, narcotics, rice, and other products smuggled to Thailand, China, and Bangladesh

Exports - commodities:

natural gas, wood products, pulses, beans, fish, rice, clothing, jade and gems

Exports - partners:

Thailand 40.5%, India 14.7%, China 14.2%, Japan 7.4% (2012)

Imports:

$7.477 billion (2012 est.)

country comparison to the world: 109

$5.921 billion (2011 est.)

note: import figures are grossly underestimated due to the value of consumer goods, diesel fuel, and other products smuggled in from Thailand, China, Malaysia, and India

Imports - commodities:

fabric, petroleum products, fertilizer, plastics, machinery, transport equipment; cement, construction materials, crude oil; food products, edible oil

Imports - partners:
China 37%, Thailand 20.2%, Singapore 8.7%, South Korea 8.7%, Japan 8.2%, Malaysia 4.6% (2012)

Reserves of foreign exchange and gold:
$7.551 billion (31 December 2012 est.)
country comparison to the world: 79
$7.017 billion (31 December 2011 est.)

Debt - external:
$5.614 billion (31 December 2012 est.)
country comparison to the world: 118
$7.766 billion (31 December 2011 est.)

Exchange rates:
kyats (MMK) per US dollar:
853.476 (2012 est.)
815 (2011 est.)
5.58 (2010 est.)
1,055 (2009)
1,205 (2008)

Fiscal year:
1 April - 31 March

Chapter 6: Energy

Electricity - production:
5.708 billion kWh (2009 est.)
country comparison to the world: 114

Electricity - consumption:
3.794 billion kWh (2009 est.)
country comparison to the world: 124

Electricity - exports:
0 kWh (2010 est.)
country comparison to the world: 167

Electricity - imports:
0 kWh (2010 est.)
country comparison to the world: 164

Electricity - installed generating capacity:
1.86 million kW (2009 est.)
country comparison to the world: 104

Electricity - from fossil fuels:
67.7% of total installed capacity (2009 est.)
country comparison to the world: 114

Electricity - from nuclear fuels:
0% of total installed capacity (2009 est.)
country comparison to the world: 53

Electricity - from hydroelectric plants:

32.3% of total installed capacity (2009 est.)

country comparison to the world: 70

Electricity - from other renewable sources:

0% of total installed capacity (2009 est.)

country comparison to the world: 112

Crude oil - production:

20,200 bbl/day (2011 est.)

country comparison to the world: 71

Crude oil - exports:

880 bbl/day (2009 est.)

country comparison to the world: 66

Crude oil - imports:

0 bbl/day (2009 est.)

country comparison to the world: 161

Crude oil - proved reserves:

50 million bbl (1 January 2012 est.)

country comparison to the world: 80

Refined petroleum products - production:

16,700 bbl/day (2008 est.)

country comparison to the world: 100

Refined petroleum products - consumption:

40,620 bbl/day (2011 est.)

country comparison to the world: 108

Refined petroleum products - exports:

0 bbl/day (2008 est.)

country comparison to the world: 156

Refined petroleum products - imports:

12,730 bbl/day (2008 est.)

country comparison to the world: 127

Natural gas - production:

12.1 billion cu m (2010 est.)

country comparison to the world: 39

Natural gas - consumption:

3.29 billion cu m (2010 est.)

country comparison to the world: 71

Natural gas - exports:

8.81 billion cu m (2010 est.)

country comparison to the world: 24

Natural gas - imports:

0 cu m (2010 est.)

country comparison to the world: 164

Natural gas - proved reserves:

283.2 billion cu m (1 January 2012 est.)

country comparison to the world: 41

Carbon dioxide emissions from consumption of energy:

12.8 million Mt (2010 est.)

country comparison to the world: 95

Chapter 7: Communications

Telephones - main lines in use:
>521,100 (2011)
>
>country comparison to the world: 96

Telephones - mobile cellular:
>1.244 million (2011)
>
>country comparison to the world: 151

Telephone system:
>general assessment: meets minimum requirements for local and intercity service for business and government
>
>domestic: system barely capable of providing basic service; mobile-cellular phone system is grossly underdeveloped
>
>international: country code - 95; landing point for the SEA-ME-WE-3 optical telecommunications submarine cable that provides links to Asia, the Middle East, and Europe; satellite earth stations - 2, Intelsat (Indian Ocean) and ShinSat (2011)

Broadcast media:
>government controls all domestic broadcast media; 2 state-controlled TV stations with 1 of the stations controlled by the armed forces; 2 pay-TV stations are

joint state-private ventures; access to satellite TV is limited; 1 state-controlled domestic radio station and 9 FM stations that are joint state-private ventures; transmissions of several international broadcasters are available in parts of Burma; the Voice of America (VOA), Radio Free Asia (RFA), BBC Burmese service, the Democratic Voice of Burma (DVB), and Radio Australia use shortwave to broadcast in Burma; VOA, RFA, and DVB produce daily TV news programs that are transmitted by satellite to audiences in Burma

Internet country code:
.mm

Internet hosts:
1,055 (2012)
country comparison to the world: 172

Internet users:
110,000 (2009)
country comparison to the world: 158

Chapter 8: Transportation

Airports:

    74 (2012)

    country comparison to the world: 73

Airports - with paved runways:

    total: 36

    over 3,047 m: 12

    2,438 to 3,047 m: 11

    1,524 to 2,437 m: 12

    under 914 m: 1 (2012)

Airports - with unpaved runways:

    total: 38

    over 3,047 m: 1

    1,524 to 2,437 m: 4

    914 to 1,523 m: 10

    under 914 m: 23 (2012)

Heliports:

    9 (2012)

Pipelines:

    gas 3,739 km; oil 551 km (2013)

Railways:

    total: 5,031 km

    country comparison to the world: 36

narrow gauge: 5,031 km 1.000-m gauge (2008)

Roadways:

total: 34,377 km (includes 358 km of expressways) (2010)

country comparison to the world: 94

Waterways:

12,800 km (2011)

country comparison to the world: 10

Merchant marine:

total: 29

country comparison to the world: 86

by type: cargo 22, passenger 2, passenger/cargo 3, specialized tanker 1, vehicle carrier 1

foreign-owned: 2 (Germany 1, Japan 1)

registered in other countries: 3 (Panama 3) (2010)

Ports and terminals:

Moulmein, Rangoon, Sittwe

Chapter 9: Military

Military branches:
> Myanmar Armed Forces (Tatmadaw): Army (Tatmadaw Kyi), Navy (Tatmadaw Yay), Air Force (Tatmadaw Lay) (2013)

Military service age and obligation:
> 18-35 years of age (men) and 18-27 years of age (women) for voluntary military service; no conscription (a 2010 law reintroducing conscription has not yet entered into force); service obligation 2 years; male (ages 18-45) and female (ages 18-35) professionals (including doctors, engineers, mechanics) serve up to 3 years; service terms may be stretched to 5 years in an officially declared emergency; Burma signed the Convention on the Rights of the Child (CRC) on 15 August 1991; on 27 June 2012, the regime signed a Joint Action Plan on prevention of child recruitment; in February 2013, the military formed a new task force to address forced child conscription, which reportedly continues (2013)

Manpower available for military service:
> males age 16-49: 14,747,845
> females age 16-49: 14,710,871 (2010 est.)

Manpower fit for military service:

males age 16-49: 10,451,515

females age 16-49: 11,181,537 (2010 est.)

Manpower reaching militarily significant age annually:

male: 522,478

female: 506,388 (2010 est.)

Military expenditures:

4.8% of GDP (2012)

country comparison to the world: 17

Chapter 10: Transnational Issues

Disputes - international:
over half of Burma's population consists of diverse ethnic groups who have substantial numbers of kin in neighboring countries; the Naf River on the border with Bangladesh serves as a smuggling and illegal transit route; Bangladesh struggles to accommodate 29,000 Rohingya, Burmese Muslim minority from Arakan State, living as refugees in Cox's Bazar; Burmese border authorities are constructing a 200 km (124 mi) wire fence designed to deter illegal cross-border transit and tensions from the military build-up along border with Bangladesh in 2010; Bangladesh referred its maritime boundary claims with Burma and India to the International Tribunal on the Law of the Sea; Burmese forces attempting to dig in to the largely autonomous Shan State to rout local militias tied to the drug trade, prompts local residents to periodically flee into neighboring Yunnan Province in China; fencing along the India-Burma international border at Manipur's Moreh town is in progress to check illegal drug trafficking and movement of militants; 140,000 mostly Karen refugees fleeing civil

strife, political upheaval and economic stagnation in Burma live in remote camps in Thailand near the border

Refugees and internally displaced persons:
IDPs: more than 454,200 (government offensives against armed ethnic minority groups near its borders with China and Thailand) (2012)

Trafficking in persons:
current situation: Burma is a source country for women, children, and men trafficked for the purpose of forced labor and commercial sexual exploitation; Burmese women and children are trafficked to East and Southeast Asia for commercial sexual exploitation, domestic servitude, and forced labor; Burmese children are subjected to conditions of forced labor in Thailand as hawkers and beggars; women are trafficked for commercial sexual exploitation to Malaysia and China; some trafficking victims transit Burma from Bangladesh to Malaysia and from China to Thailand; Burma's internal trafficking remains the most serious concern occurring primarily from villages to urban centers and economic hubs for labor in industrial zones, agricultural estates, and commercial sexual

exploitation; the Burmese military continues to engage in the unlawful conscription of child soldiers, and continues to be the main perpetrator of forced labor inside Burma; a small number of foreign pedophiles occasionally exploit Burmese children in the country

tier rating: Tier 3 - the driving factors behind Burma's significant trafficking problem are the regime's gross economic mismanagement and human rights abuses, the military's continued widespread use of forced and child labor, and the recruitment of child soldiers; although the government of Burma has taken some steps to address cross-border sex trafficking, it has not demonstrated serious and sustained efforts to clamp down on military and local authorities who are themselves deriving economic benefit from forced labor practices (2010)

Illicit drugs:

world's third largest producer of illicit opium with an estimated production in 2009 of 250 metric tons, a decrease of 27%, and poppy cultivation in 2009 totaled 17,000 hectares, a 24% decrease from 2008; production in the United Wa State Army's areas of greatest control remains low; Shan state is the source of 94.5% of Burma's poppy cultivation; lack of government will to take on major narcotrafficking groups and lack of serious commitment against money laundering continues to hinder the overall antidrug effort; major source of methamphetamine and heroin for regional consumption (2008)

Map of Myanmar (Burma)

Other Key Facts™ Titles

Key Facts on Syria

Key Facts on China

Key Facts on Qatar

Key Facts on India

Key Facts on Germany

Key Facts on Argentina

Key Facts on Russia

Key Facts on North Korea

Key Facts on Brazil

Key Facts on Italy

Key Facts on the United Arab Emirates

Key Facts on the European Union

Key Facts on Pakistan

Key Facts on Saudi Arabia

Key Facts on Cyprus

Key Facts on Iran

Key Facts on Afghanistan

Key Facts on Iraq

Key Facts on Indonesia

Key Facts on South Korea

Key Facts on France

Key Facts on the United Kingdom

Key Facts on Egypt

Key Facts on Israel

Key Facts on Mexico

Key Facts on the United States of America

Key Facts on Turkey

Key Facts on South Africa

Key Facts on Greece

Key Facts on Japan

Key Facts on Malaysia

Key Facts on Vietnam

Key Facts on Hong Kong

Key Facts on Jordan

Key Facts on Australia

Key Facts on Venezuela

All Key Facts™ Titles are Available at

www.Amazon.com

THE INTERNATIONALIST®

2013

WWW.INTERNATIONALIST.COM

www.ingramcontent.com/pod-product-compliance
Lightning Source LLC
Chambersburg PA
CBHW071642170526
45166CB00003B/1399